and in... *ko Sunajko*

GOOD KNIGHT, SLEEP TIGHT
by David Melling

A catalogue record of this book is available from
the British Library.
ISBN 978-0-340-86093-9

First edition published 2006
10 9 8 7

Published by Hodder Children's Books
338 Euston Road London NW1 3BH

Hodder Children's Books Australia
Level 17/207 Kent Street
Sydney NSW 2000

Printed in China

Hodder Children's Books
is a division of Hachette
Children's Books
An Hachette Livre UK Company

GOOD KNIGHT
SLEEP TIGHT

written and illustrated by

DAVID MELLING

A division of Hachette Children's Books

A NEW SOUND
echoed along the
corridors of the castle.
To the king and queen
was born a
royal princess.

The prince
had a baby sister.

He couldn't see what all the fuss was about.

Among the many
splendid presents was
the softest, fluffiest pillow
in the kingdom.

But one day
the fat royal cat
squashed it flat!

The poor princess cried.

And cried.

And cried.

So the king popped over for a
little chat with his loyal knight.

**'Fill this with something
soft and fluffy!'** he barked.

'And hurry!'

The knight leapt into action.

He was so quick there wasn't even enough time to finish the senten

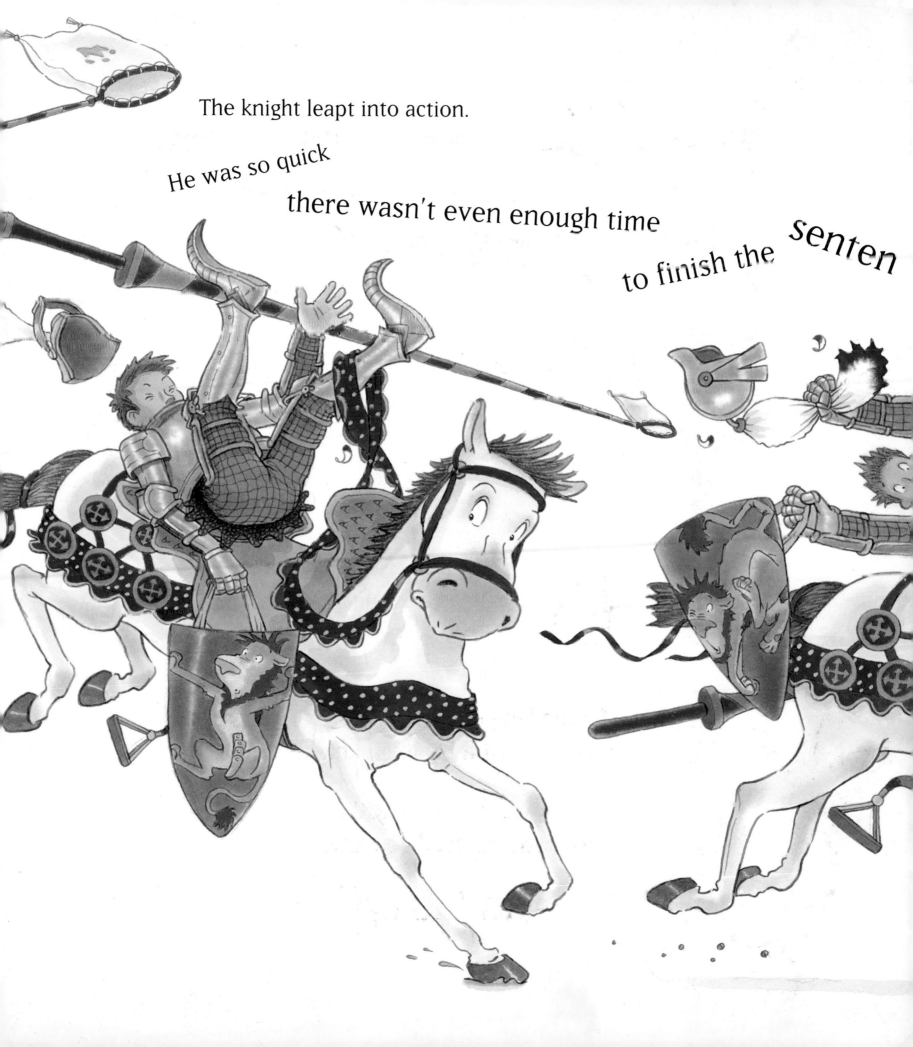

Deep inside the wild wood prickly bears rubbed their grumbly tummies. 'Lunch time!' they slurped.

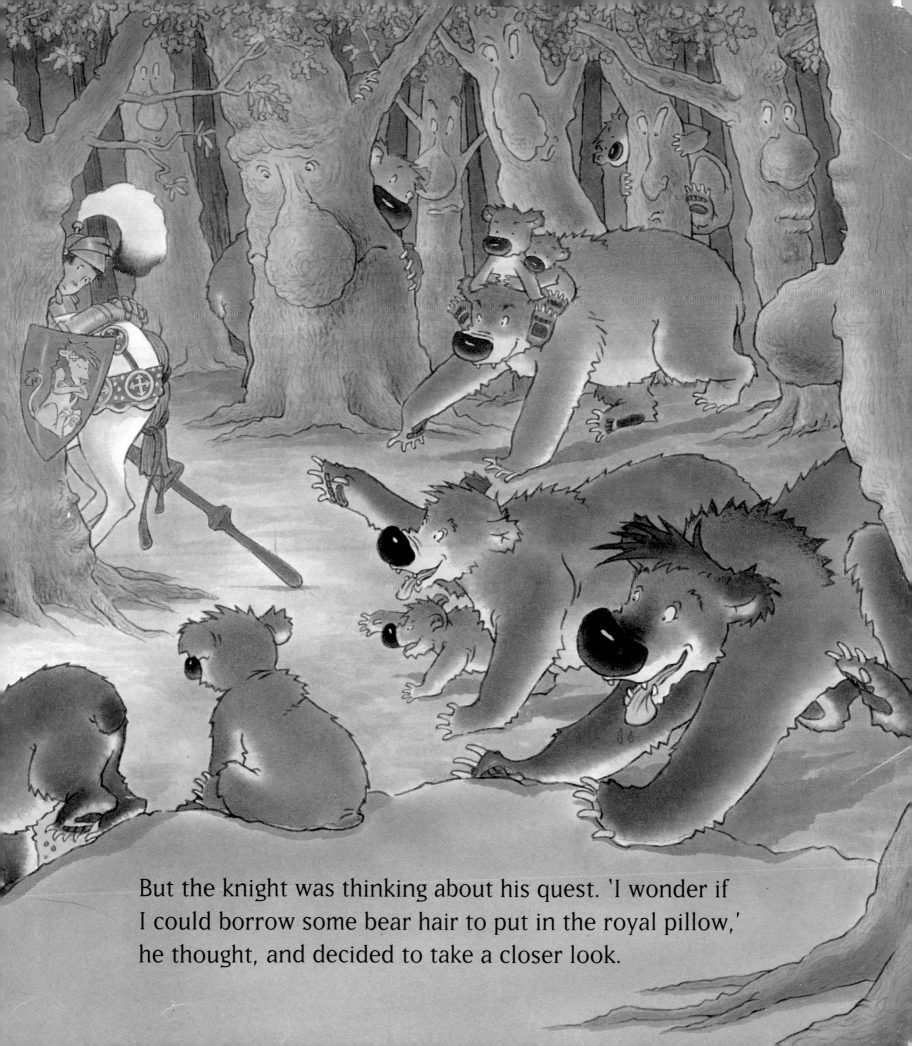

But the knight was thinking about his quest. 'I wonder if I could borrow some bear hair to put in the royal pillow,' he thought, and decided to take a closer look.

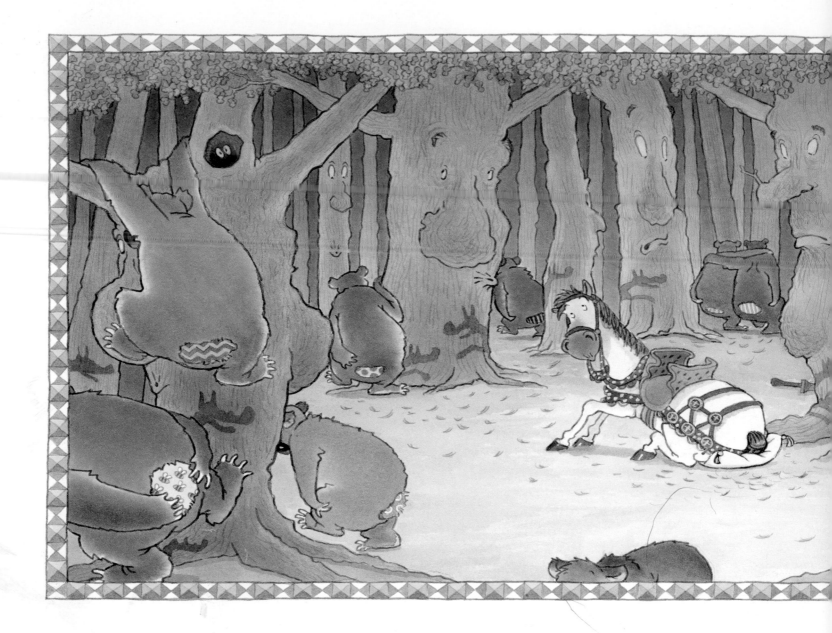

Two minutes later the grizzled bears shuffled back into the shadows, rubbing their sore bottoms and mumbling to themselves.

'Well really, it's hardly fair. We just wanted a quick nibble. No need for that ...'

Bear hair lay everywhere!

The knight filled the pillow and gave it to the horse.
'Is this pillow soft enough for the princess?' he asked.
'Neigh!' said the horse. (He thought it was too scratchy.)

Nobody noticed slinky shadows curling around the
tree trunks.

A jumble of wolves howwwled from the trees — they sniffed the knight, they sniffed the horse, then sniffed off.

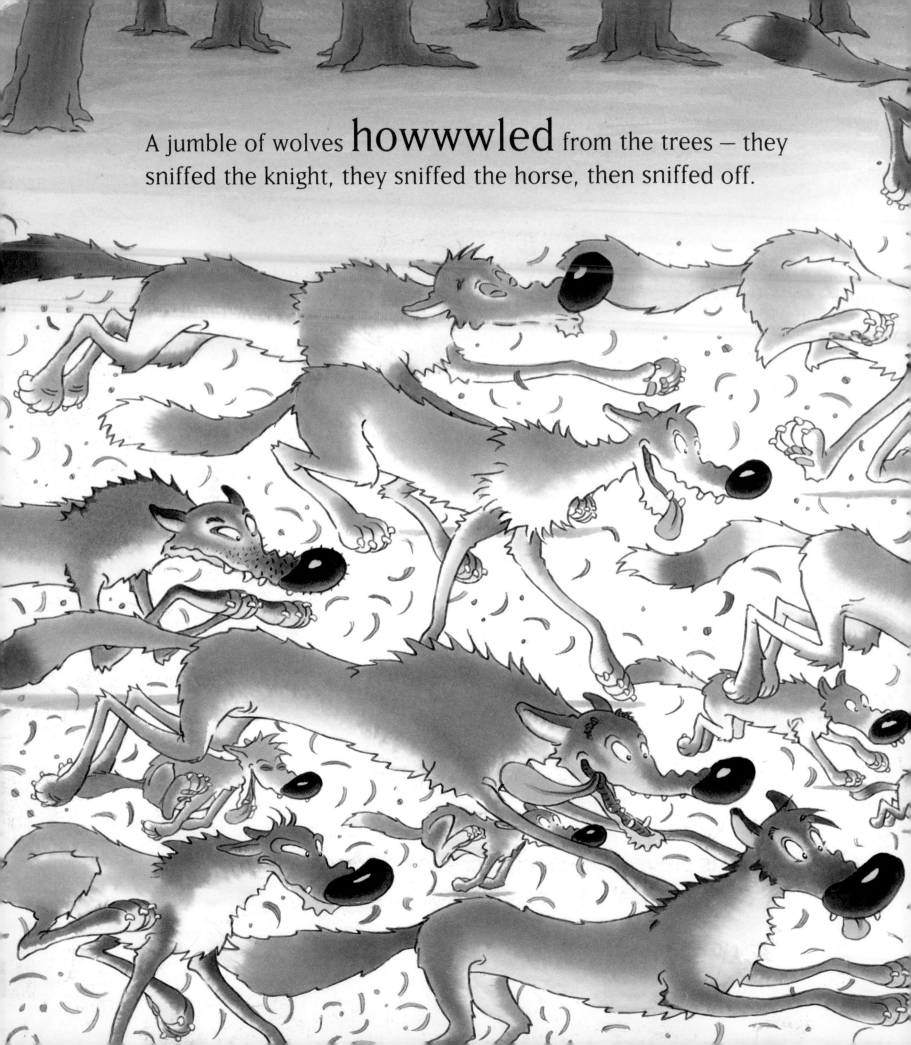

Wolf hair lay everywhere!

The knight filled the pillow again and gave it to the horse.
'Is **this** pillow soft enough for the princess?' he asked.
'Neigh!' said the horse. (He thought it was too bristly.)

Just then...

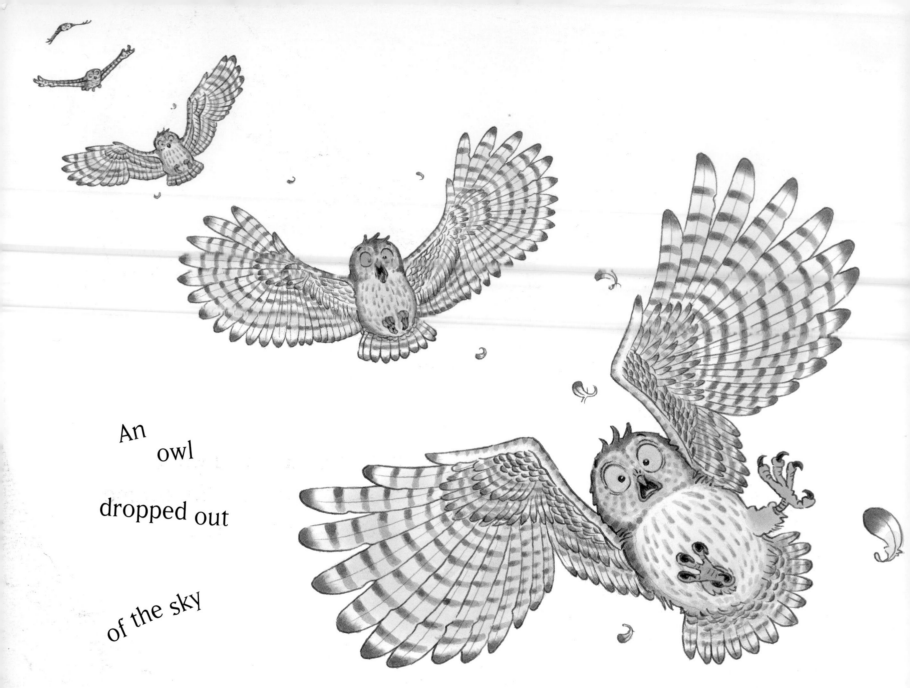

An owl

dropped out

of the sky

and bounced off the knight's head.

Feathers fluttered gently to the floor.

'That's it!' cried the knight.
'I'll make a pillow of feathers!'

'If it's feathers you want,'
said the dizzy owl, 'follow me.
I'll take you to see …

...the Feather Trees!'

So the knight and his **'I'm COMPLETELY scared of heights'** horse clambered up into the branches.

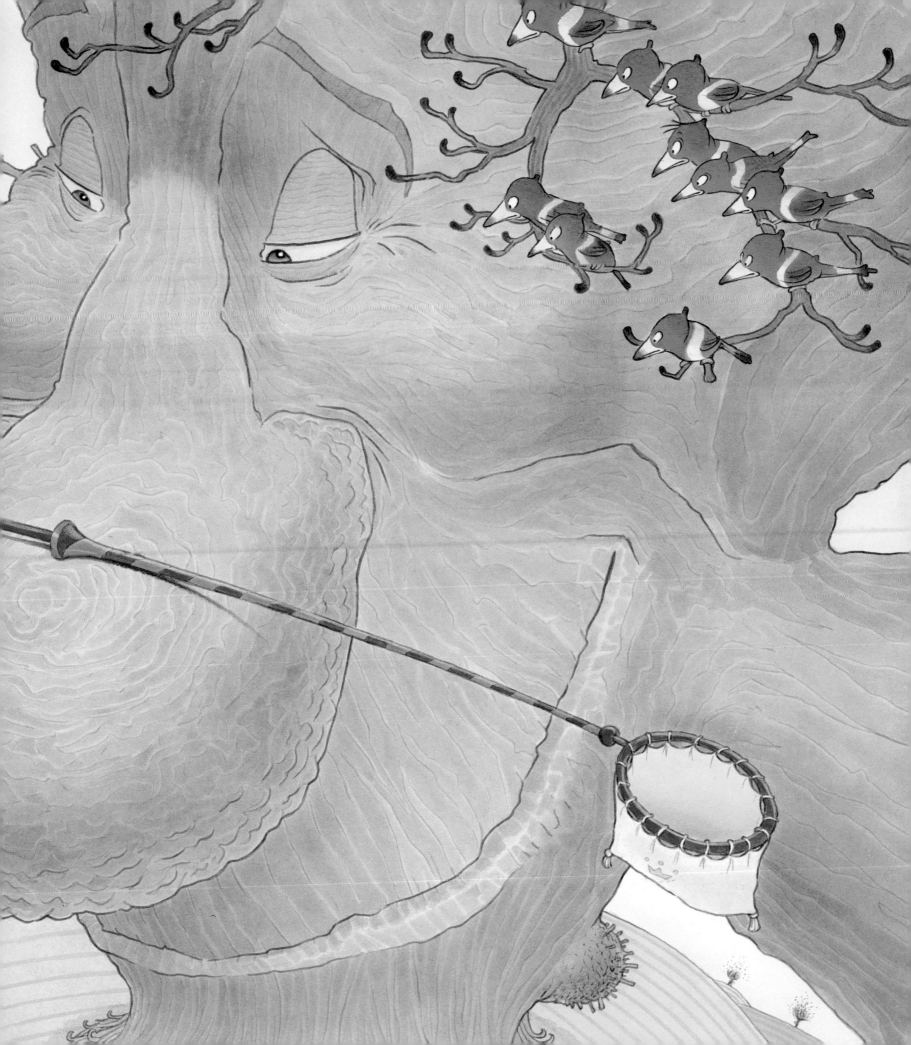

All the birds gathered round to listen
to the knight's tale. There were feathers
everywhere!

When he had finished, the birds happily agreed
to help and plucked just enough feathers to fill
the pillow to the royal brim.

The knight and his faithful horse waved goodbye and galloped and galloped and galloped until they came back to the wild wood.

They wrestled and wriggled their way through its darkest secrets …

...and  out the other side.

No one in the castle had slept for a week so they were jolly pleased to see the knight return.

'Place that child upon that pillow before I go **bananas!**'

wailed the king.

Everyone held their breath ...

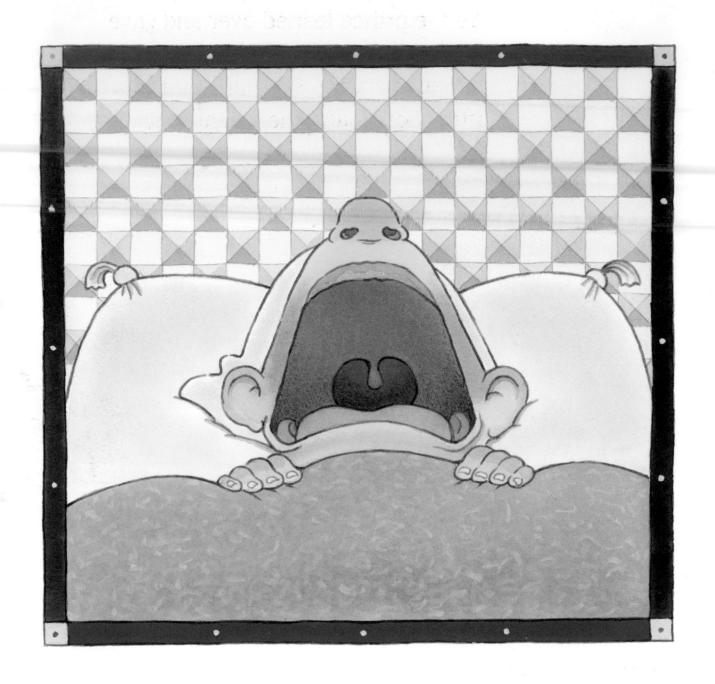

The princess didn't!

So the prince leaned over and gave his baby sister a cuddle. The princess stopped crying. She smiled, blew a little bubble, and then went to sleep.

The king hugged the prince.

The queen hugged the prince.

At last the castle fell silent …

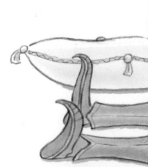

…except for the snoring that snuffled,

sleepily through the corridors.

Good knight, sleep tight.